Decoding the TOEFL® iBT

Basic

SPEAKING

INTRODUCTION

For many learners of English, the TOEFL® iBT will be the most important standardized test they ever take. Unfortunately for a large number of these individuals, the material covered on the TOEFL® iBT remains a mystery to them, so they are unable to do well on the test. We hope that by using the *Decoding the TOEFL® iBT* series, individuals who take the TOEFL® iBT will be able to excel on the test and, in the process of using the book, may unravel the mysteries of the test and therefore make the material covered on the TOEFL® iBT more familiar to themselves.

The TOEFL® iBT covers the four main skills that a person must learn when studying any foreign language: reading, listening, speaking, and writing. The *Decoding the TOEFL® iBT* series contains books that cover all four of these skills. The *Decoding the TOEFL® iBT* series contains books with three separate levels for all four of the topics as well as the *Decoding the TOEFL® iBT Actual Test* books. These books are all designed to enable learners to utilize them to become better prepared to take the TOEFL® iBT. This book, *Decoding the TOEFL® iBT Speaking Basic*, covers the speaking aspect of the test. It is designed to help learners prepare for the Speaking section of the TOEFL® iBT.

Decoding the TOEFL® iBT Speaking Basic can be used by learners who are taking classes and also by individuals who are studying by themselves. It contains three parts and forty units. Part A covers the Independent Speaking Task (Question 1) while Part B and Part C cover the Integrated Speaking Tasks (Questions 2-4). There is also one actual test at the end of the book. Each unit has either two independent questions or two integrated questions. It also contains exercises designed to help learners understand how to present the best possible responses for the Speaking section. The passages and questions in *Decoding the TOEFL® iBT Speaking Basic* are lower levels than those found on the TOEFL® iBT. Individuals who use *Decoding the TOEFL® iBT Speaking Basic* will therefore be able to prepare themselves not only to take the TOEFL® iBT but also to perform well on the test.

We hope that everyone who uses *Decoding the TOEFL® iBT Speaking Basic* will be able to become more familiar with the TOEFL® iBT and will additionally improve his or her score on the test. As the title of the book implies, we hope that learners can use it to crack the code on the TOEFL® iBT, to make the test itself less mysterious and confusing, and to get the highest grade possible. Finally, we hope that both learners and instructors can use this book to its full potential. We wish all of you the best of luck as you study English and prepare for the TOEFL® iBT, and we hope that *Decoding the TOEFL® iBT Speaking Basic* can provide you with assistance during the course of your studies.

Michael A. Putlack
Stephen Poirier
Tony Covello

TABLE
OF
CONTENTS

ABOUT THE TOEFL® iBT SPEAKING SECTION

How the Section Is Organized

The Speaking section is the third part of the TOEFL® iBT and consists of four questions. Question 1 is called the Independent Speaking Task and asks test takers to speak about a familiar topic. The other questions, questions 2-4, are called the Integrated Speaking Tasks. These tasks require test takers to integrate their speaking skills with other language skills such as listening and reading skills.

For each of the four questions, test takers are given preparation time and response time. During the preparation time, test takers can write down brief notes about how they will organize their responses. The preparation time ranges from 15 to 30 seconds, and the response time is either 45 or 60 seconds. The spoken responses are recorded and sent to be scored by raters. The raters evaluate responses based on three criteria: Delivery (how clear your speech is), Language Use (how effectively you use grammar and vocabulary to convey your ideas), and Topic Development (how fully you answer the question and how coherently you present your ideas).

Changes in the Speaking Section

The Speaking section is the section that has gone through the most drastic changes. Two question types – Questions 1 and 5 on the old test – have been removed. Therefore, the total number of questions has become four instead of six. Accordingly, the time allotted for the Speaking section has been reduced from 20 minutes to 17 minutes. However, the remaining questions have no changes, and the preparation times and the response times remain the same.

Question Types

TYPE 1 Independent Speaking Task: Question 1

The first question asks test takers to speak about a familiar topic. It is necessary for test takers to include specific examples and details in their response. After the question is presented, test takers are given 15 seconds to prepare their response and 45 seconds to speak.

Question 1 asks test takers to make a personal choice between two possible opinions, actions, or situations. In addition, on recent tests, test takers are sometimes given three options from which to choose, and they may be asked to speak about both the advantages and the disadvantages of a particular topic. Test takers are required to explain their choice by providing reasons and details. Topics for this question include everyday issues of general interest to test takers. For example, the question may ask about a preference between studying at home and studying at the library, a preference between living in a dormitory and living in an off-campus apartment, or a preference between a class with a lot of discussion and one without discussion.

ABOUT THE TOEFL® iBT SPEAKING SECTION

TYPE 2 **Integrated Speaking Tasks** (Reading, Listening, and Speaking): **Questions 2 and 3**

The second and third questions require test takers to integrate different language skills. Test takers are first presented with a short reading passage. The time given for reading is 45-50 seconds. After that, test takers will listen to a conversation or a lecture which is related to information presented in the reading passage. They need to organize their response by using information from both the reading passage and the conversation or lecture. For these questions, test takers are given 30 seconds to prepare their response and 60 seconds to speak.

Question 2 concerns a topic of campus-related interest, but it does not require prior firsthand experience of college or university life in North America to understand the topic. The reading passage is usually between 75 and 100 words long. It may be an announcement, letter, or article regarding a policy, rule, or future plan of a college or university. It can also be related to campus facilities or the quality of life on campus. After reading the passage, test takers will listen to two speakers discuss the topic presented in the reading passage. Typically, one of the two speakers shows a strong opinion about the topic. On recent tests, however, speakers have shown mixed feelings about the topic, so they like it yet also dislike some aspect of it. Test takers need to summarize the speaker's opinion and the reasons for holding it.

In Question 3, test takers will read a short passage about an academic subject and then listen to a professor lecture about that subject. The question requires test takers to relate the reading passage and the lecture. Topics for this question can be drawn from a variety of fields, including life science, social science, physical science, and the humanities. However, the question does not require prior knowledge of any particular field.

TYPE 3 **Integrated Speaking Task** (Listening and Speaking): **Question 4**

The last question presents only a listening passage—a lecture—and not a reading passage. Test takers need to respond based on what they hear. They are given 20 seconds to prepare their response and 60 seconds to speak.

For Question 4, test takers will listen to a lecture about an academic topic. As in Question 3, topics for this question can be drawn from a variety of fields, including life science, social science, physical science, and the humanities. Again, no prior knowledge is necessary to understand the lecture. After hearing the lecture, test takers are asked to summarize the lecture and to explain how the examples are connected with the overall topic.

HOW TO USE THIS BOOK

Decoding the TOEFL® iBT Speaking Basic is designed to be used either as a textbook in a classroom environment or as a study guide for individual learners. There are 3 parts and 40 units in this book. Each unit provides 2 sample questions, which enable you to build up your skills on a particular speaking task. At the end of the book, there is one actual test of the Speaking section of the TOEFL® iBT.

 Part A   **Independent Speaking Task**

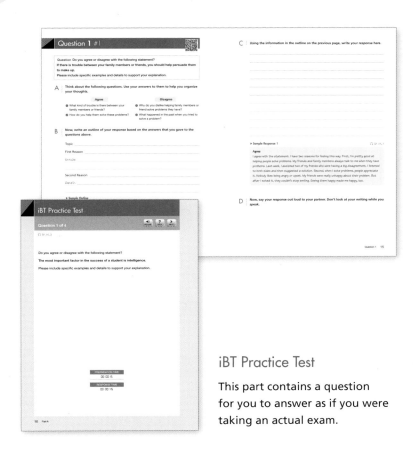

This section has brainstorming questions and spaces to write an outline and a sample answer. A sample outline and a sample response are provided to help you write your own.

iBT Practice Test

This part contains a question for you to answer as if you were taking an actual exam.

Part B · Integrated Speaking Tasks: Reading, Listening, and Speaking

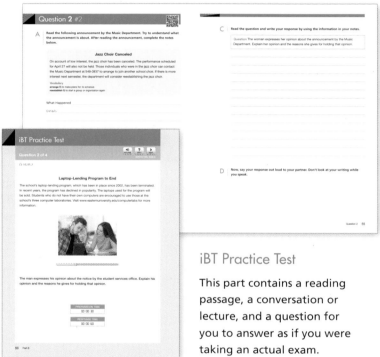

This part has a reading passage followed by either a conversation or lecture. There are spaces to take notes on the passage and the conversation or lecture. This is followed by a space to write your own sample answer.

iBT Practice Test

This part contains a reading passage, a conversation or lecture, and a question for you to answer as if you were taking an actual exam.

Part C · Integrated Speaking Task: Listening and Speaking

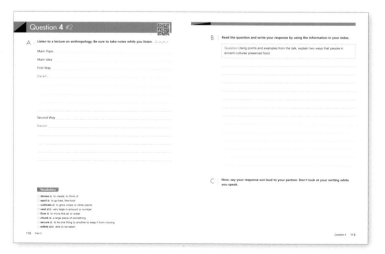

This part has a lecture. There is space to take notes on the lecture. This is followed by a space to write your own sample answer.

iBT Practice Test

This part contains a lecture and a question for you to answer as if you were taking an actual exam.

Actual Test (at the end of the book)

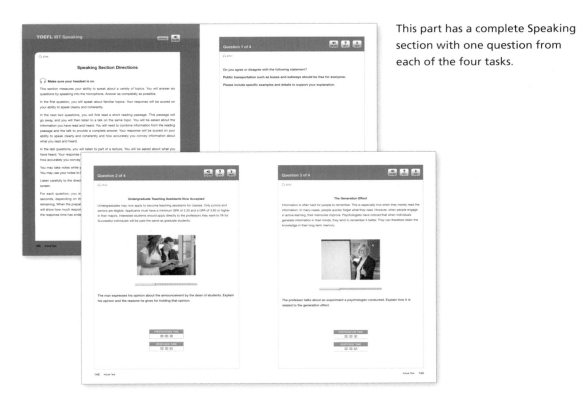

This part has a complete Speaking section with one question from each of the four tasks.

Part A

Independent Speaking Task
Question 1

Independent Speaking Task

◢ About the Task

The Independent Speaking Task asks test takers to speak about familiar topics. It is necessary for test takers to include specific examples and details in their response. After the question is presented, test takers are given 15 seconds to prepare their response and 45 seconds to speak.

The Independent Speaking Task is the first question (question 1) of the Speaking section.

Question 1 asks test takers to make a personal choice between two or three possible opinions, actions, or situations. Test takers are required to explain their choice by providing reasons and details. Topics for this question include everyday issues of general interest to test takers. For example, the question may ask about a preference between studying at home and studying at the library, a preference between living in a dormitory and living in an off-campus apartment, or a preference between a class with a lot of discussion and one without discussion.

When you answer the question, be sure to use examples. Personal examples involving family members are ideal. The examples you use do not have to be actual events that occurred, but you should present them that way. You merely need to provide examples that defend the argument you are making. In addition, do not discuss both sides for the question. Make your choice and speak only about it.

■ Sample Question

🎧 Q1_00_1

Do you agree or disagree with the following statement?

These days, people use their smartphones too much.

Please include specific examples and details to support your explanation.

PREPARATION TIME
00:00:15

RESPONSE TIME
00:00:45

Sample Response   🎧 Q1_00_2

I agree with this statement very much. Most of my friends can't seem to put their smartphones down. As a result, it negatively affects their lives. First, my friends even use their smartphones during class, so they don't listen to their teachers talk. This prevents them from learning. Another problem is that people's monthly smartphone bills are too high. Some of my friends constantly watch movies and play games on their phones. So they have to pay huge amounts of money every month. They usually can't afford it, so they have to ask their parents for money.

Question Do you agree or disagree with the following statement?

If there is trouble between your family members or friends, you should help persuade them to make up.

Please include specific examples and details to support your explanation.

A **Think about the following questions. Use your answers to them to help you organize your thoughts.**

Agree	Disagree
❶ What kind of trouble is there between your family members or friends?	❶ Why do you dislike helping family members or friend solve problems they have?
❷ How do you help them solve these problems?	❷ What happened in the past when you tried to solve a problem?

B **Now, write an outline of your response based on the answers that you gave to the questions above.**

Topic _____

First Reason _____

Details _____

_____

Second Reason _____

Details _____

_____

▶ Sample Outline

Topic	Agree
First Reason	good at helping people solve problems
Details	- people talk to me when have problems - helped 2 friends last week → listened and then proposed solution
Second Reason	when solve problems, people appreciate it
Details	- nobody likes being angry or upset - friends were upset → smiled after solved problem

C | **Using the information in the outline on the previous page, write your response here.**

_____

_____

_____

_____

_____

_____

_____

_____

_____

_____

▶ **Sample Response 1**   🎧 Q1_01_1

> **Agree**
> I agree with the statement. I have two reasons for feeling this way. First, I'm pretty good at helping people solve problems. My friends and family members always talk to me when they have problems. Last week, I assisted two of my friends who were having a big disagreement. I listened to both sides and then suggested a solution. Second, when I solve problems, people appreciate it. Nobody likes being angry or upset. My friends were really unhappy about their problem. But after I solved it, they couldn't stop smiling. Seeing them happy made me happy, too.

D | **Now, say your response out loud to your partner. Don't look at your writing while you speak.**

iBT Practice Test

🎧 Q1_01_3

Do you agree or disagree with the following statement?

The most important factor in the success of a student is intelligence.

Please include specific examples and details to support your explanation.

PREPARATION TIME
00:00:15

RESPONSE TIME
00:00:45

Question 1 #2

Question Some people like to use smartphones or other navigational devices to guide them while they are driving. Others prefer to ask people for directions. Which do you prefer and why? Please include specific examples and details to support your explanation.

A | **Think about the following questions. Use your answers to them to help you organize your thoughts.**

Using Smartphones or Other Navigational Devices	Asking People for Directions
❶ Why do you prefer to use smartphones or other navigational devices?	❶ Why do you prefer not to use smartphones or navigational devices?
❷ How often do you go to places you have never visited before?	❷ How comfortable are you talking to strangers?

B | **Now, write an outline of your response based on the answers that you gave to the questions above.**

Your Choice _____

First Reason _____

Details _____

_____

Second Reason _____

Details _____

_____

▶ Sample Outline

Your Choice	Using Smartphones or Other Navigational Devices
First Reason	show where to go and how to get there
Details	- visited uncle in other city last week - device showed where to go
Second Reason	can tell about distance to destination and traffic
Details	- mom uses device - avoids traffic jams when commuting

C | **Using the information in the outline on the previous page, write your response here.**

_____

_____

_____

_____

_____

_____

_____

_____

_____

_____

▶ Sample Response 1   🎧 Q1_02_1

Using Smartphones or Other Navigational Devices

Using a smartphone or other navigational devices while driving is better than asking for directions. First, these electronic devices show exactly where you need to go and how to get there. Last week, my family drove to another city to visit my uncle. We didn't know where his house was, but the navigational device in our car showed us where to go. Second, electronic devices can tell how far away your destination is and how bad traffic on the roads is. My mother uses a navigational device to avoid traffic jams when she commutes to work and home.

D | **Now, say your response out loud to your partner. Don't look at your writing while you speak.**

🎧 Q1_02_3

Some people like to visit places in person. Others prefer to see documentaries of different places. Which do you prefer and why? Please include specific examples and details to support your explanation.

PREPARATION TIME
00:00:15

RESPONSE TIME
00:00:45

Question Do you agree or disagree with the following statement?

Schools should record teachers' lectures and put them on their websites.

Please include specific examples and details to support your explanation.

A | **Think about the following questions. Use your answers to them to help you organize your thoughts.**

Agree	Disagree
❶ How can putting lectures online help students?	❶ What are some disadvantages to putting lectures online?
❷ How can teachers improve if their lectures are online?	❷ Why might teachers dislike having their lectures be online?

B | **Now, write an outline of your response based on the answers that you gave to the questions above.**

Your Choice _____

First Reason _____

Details _____

_____

Second Reason _____

Details _____

_____

▶ Sample Outline

Your Choice	Agree
First Reason	could help students
Details	- can't write fast → notes aren't good - if see lectures online, can take good notes
Second Reason	parents can see what children learning
Details	- can watch lectures - determine if teachers are good or bad

C | Using the information in the outline on the previous page, write your response here.

_____

_____

_____

_____

_____

_____

_____

_____

_____

_____

▶ Sample Response 1   🎧 Q1_03_1

Agree

I strongly agree with the statement for two reasons. The first is that putting lectures online could help the students. For example, I always pay attention in class, but I can't write fast. That means my notes aren't good because I can't write down everything my teachers say. If I could see my teachers' lectures online, I could make excellent notes. The second reason is that parents should be able to see what their children are learning. They can watch the lectures and determine if the teachers are good or bad. My parents would love to do that.

D | Now, say your response out loud to your partner. Don't look at your writing while you speak.

🎧 Q1_03_3

Do you agree or disagree with the following statement?

Students need to do homework during summer vacation.

Please include specific examples and details to support your explanation.

PREPARATION TIME
00:00:15

RESPONSE TIME
00:00:45

Question Which would you prefer, to get feedback from a teacher in writing or to get feedback from a teacher in person? Why do you feel that way? Please include specific examples and details to support your explanation.

A | **Think about the following questions. Use your answers to them to help you organize your thoughts.**

Get Feedback in Writing	Get Feedback in Person
❶ Why do you prefer to get feedback from a teacher in writing?	❶ Why do you prefer to get feedback from a teacher in person?
❷ Why do teachers prefer to give written feedback?	❷ Why do teachers prefer to give spoken feedback?

B | **Now, write an outline of your response based on the answers that you gave to the questions above.**

Your Choice _____

First Reason _____

Details _____

_____

Second Reason _____

Details _____

_____

▶ Sample Outline

Your Choice	Get Feedback in Writing
First Reason	can read again and again
Details	- won't forget - teacher does this → understand how wants me to improve
Second Reason	can show feedback to others
Details	- ask if they agree w/it - ask to contribute → friend made suggestion to teacher's feedback

C | **Using the information in the outline on the previous page, write your response here.**

_____

_____

_____

_____

_____

_____

_____

_____

_____

_____

_____

▶ **Sample Response 1** 🎧 Q1_04_1

Get Feedback in Writing

If I had to choose, I'd prefer to get feedback from a teacher in writing. First, if the teacher writes down advice, I can read everything again and again. That way, I won't forget it. One of my teachers gives feedback this way. I therefore easily understand how she wants me to improve. Second, I can show written feedback to others and ask if they agree with it. I can also ask if they can contribute to the teacher's feedback. My best friend made a suggestion to some feedback I received in history class. Thanks to him, my work improved.

D | **Now, say your response out loud to your partner. Don't look at your writing while you speak.**

Q1_04_3

Which would you prefer, attending a college in your hometown or going to a university in a different city? Why do you want to do that? Please include specific examples and details to support your explanation.

PREPARATION TIME
00:00:15

RESPONSE TIME
00:00:45

> **Question** Do you agree or disagree with the following statement?
>
> **High school students should learn how to cook at school.**
>
> Please include specific examples and details to support your explanation.

A | **Think about the following questions. Use your answers to them to help you organize your thoughts.**

Agree	**Disagree**
❶ Why should high school students learn to cook at school?	❶ Why don't you think high school students should learn to cook at school?
❷ What skills can the students learn?	❷ How should students learn to cook?

B | **Now, write an outline of your response based on the answers that you gave to the questions above.**

Your Choice _____

First Reason _____

Details _____

_____

Second Reason _____

Details _____

_____

▶ **Sample Outline**

Your Choice	Agree
First Reason	cooking = important skill
Details	- sister took cooking class → lives alone now - cooks every night → happy she took class
Second Reason	practice skills learned in other classes
Details	- measure amounts and mix ingredients - use skills learned in math and science → get practical experience

C | **Using the information in the outline on the previous page, write your response here.**

_____

_____

_____

_____

_____

_____

_____

_____

_____

_____

▶ Sample Response 1   🎧 Q1_05_1

Agree

I agree with this statement for two reasons. The first is that cooking is an important skill everyone should learn. My sister took a cooking class in high school. She lives alone now and cooks almost every night. She said she's so happy she took the class because she can prepare her own meals. The second is that students can practice skills learned in other classes in cooking class. For instance, cooking requires people to measure amounts and to mix ingredients. These are skills students learn in math and science classes. So a cooking class would give students practical experience.

D | **Now, say your response out loud to your partner. Don't look at your writing while you speak.**

Q1_05_3

Do you agree or disagree with the following statement?

Having a lot of free time is good for you.

Please include specific examples and details to support your explanation.

PREPARATION TIME
00:00:15

RESPONSE TIME
00:00:45

Question Imagine that you are going to live in a dormitory at your school. Which of the following places would you prefer to live?

- A dormitory with small rooms but which has the latest facilities
- A dormitory with old rooms but which is historically famous
- A dormitory with single rooms but which costs a lot of money

Use details and examples to explain your answer.

A Think about the following questions. Use your answers to them to help you organize your thoughts.

❶ What will you use your dormitory room for?

❷ What facilities in a dormitory are important to you?

❸ What would you like about living in an historical building?

❹ What are some benefits of not having any roommates?

❺ How important is the price of a dormitory room to you?

B Now, write an outline of your response based on the answers that you gave to the questions above.

Your Choice _____

First Reason _____

Details _____

_____

Second Reason _____

Details _____

Your Choice	Small Rooms and the Latest Facilities
First Reason	be in dorm room to sleep
Details	- don't care if room is small - need bed, wardrobe, and bookshelf
Second Reason	want modern facilities
Details	- gym, cafeteria, and lounge = great - dorm life would be comfortable

C | Using the information in the outline above, write your response here.

_____

_____

_____

_____

_____

_____

_____

_____

_____

_____

▶ Sample Response 1   🎧 Q1_06_1

Small Rooms and the Latest Facilities

I would prefer to live in a dormitory with small rooms and the latest facilities. First of all, I will only be in my dormitory room to sleep. So I don't care if the room is small. I only need a bed, a wardrobe for my clothes, and a bookshelf. Secondly, I would love to have modern facilities in my dormitory. A gym would be great. So would a cafeteria and a lounge. Facilities like them would make living in the dormitory more comfortable. I definitely want to stay in that kind of dormitory.

D | Now, say your response out loud to your partner. Don't look at your writing while you speak.

iBT Practice Test

🎧 Q1_06_3

Imagine that you are going to do some volunteer work on the weekend. Which of the following volunteer work would you prefer to do?

• Work at an animal shelter

• Volunteer at a hospital

• Help clean up a local park

Use details and examples to explain your answer.

PREPARATION TIME
00:00:15

RESPONSE TIME
00:00:45

Question Answer one of the following questions.

1 Some people prefer to educate children by emphasizing competition while others prefer to avoid having any kind of competition between students. Talk about the advantages and disadvantages of educating children by emphasizing competition. Use details and examples to explain your answer.

2 Some people prefer to educate children by emphasizing competition while others prefer to avoid having any kind of competition between students. Talk about the advantages and disadvantages of educating children by avoiding having any kind of competition between students. Use details and examples to explain your answer.

A | **Think about the following questions. Use your answers to them to help you organize your thoughts.**

❶ Why are children competitive?

❷ How can competition benefit children?

❸ How can children be hurt by competition?

❹ How can children motivate themselves to do better?

B | **Now, write an outline of your response based on the answers that you gave to the questions above.**

Topic _____

Advantages _____

_____

Disadvantages _____

_____

▶ **Sample Outline**

Topic	Emphasizing Competition
Advantages	- students want to win → try harder - competition brings out the best in people → do better competing against others
Disadvantages	- get upset when lose → friend cries when she doesn't win - children become self-centered → don't care about others

C | Using the information in the outline above, write your response here.

_____

_____

_____

_____

_____

_____

_____

_____

_____

_____

▶ **Sample Response 1** 🎧 Q1_07_1

Emphasizing Competition

Emphasizing competition between students has some advantages. One is that students will try harder because they want to win. I always try my best when competing against others. Another reason is that competition brings out the best in people. When I'm competing, I always do better than when I'm doing an activity alone. However, there are also disadvantages. Some people get upset when they lose. My friend sometimes cries if she doesn't win a competition. A second reason is that some children become self-centered. They try to win every competition and don't care about anybody else.

D | Now, say your response out loud to your partner. Don't look at your writing while you speak.

🎧 Q1_07_3

Answer one of the following questions.

1   Some students prefer having face-to-face meetings with their teachers while others prefer to have online meetings. Talk about the advantages and disadvantages of having face-to-face meetings. Use details and examples to explain your answer.

2   Some students prefer having face-to-face meetings with their teachers while others prefer to have online meetings. Talk about the advantages and disadvantages of having online meetings. Use details and examples to explain your answer.

PREPARATION TIME
00:00:15

RESPONSE TIME
00:00:45

Question 1 #8

> **Question** Which of the following should students do during their summer vacations?
>
> • Take extra classes at school or a private academy
>
> • Get a part-time job
>
> • Go on a trip with their family
>
> Use details and examples to explain your answer.

A | Think about the following questions. Use your answers to them to help you organize your thoughts.

Take Extra Classes	Get a Part-Time Job	Go on a Trip
❶ Why would you like to study more?	❶ What kind of job would you like to get?	❶ Where would you like to go on a trip?
❷ What subjects would you like to study?	❷ What can you learn at a part-time job?	❷ What would you like to do on the trip?

B | Now, write an outline of your response based on the answers that you gave to the questions above.

Your Choice _____

First Reason _____

Details _____

_____

Second Reason _____

Details _____

_____

Your Choice	Get a Part-Time Job
First Reason	provide work experience
Details	- bro had part-time job → plenty of experience - graduated from college → hired by top company
Second Reason	can learn responsibility
Details	- have duties → become more responsible - parents were happy w/bro → always did chores

C | **Using the information in the outline above, write your response here.**

▶ **Sample Response 1** 🎧 Q1_08_1

Get a Part-Time Job

In my opinion, students should get part-time jobs during their summer vacations. First, a job will provide work experience. This will help them in the future. My older brother always had part-time summer jobs. After graduating from college, he had plenty of job experience. So he got hired by a top company. Secondly, a person can learn responsibility at a job. By having many duties, a person can become more responsible. That happened to my brother. My parents were happy because he always did his chores at home. He became very responsible thanks to his part-time jobs.

D | **Now, say your response out loud to your partner. Don't look at your writing while you speak.**

🎧 Q1_08_3

Which of the following should elementary school students be required to do?

• Participate in team sports
• Study either art or music
• Join a school club

Use details and examples to explain your answer.

PREPARATION TIME
00:00:15

RESPONSE TIME
00:00:45

> **Question** Answer one of the following questions.
>
> **1** Some parents prefer to let their children make mistakes when they are learning something new while others prefer to correct their children's mistakes at once. Talk about the advantages and disadvantages of letting children make mistakes while learning. Use details and examples to explain your answer.
>
> **2** Some parents prefer to let their children make mistakes when they are learning something new while others prefer to correct their children's mistakes at once. Talk about the advantages and disadvantages of correcting children's mistakes at once while learning. Use details and examples to explain your answer.

A Think about the following questions. Use your answers to them to help you organize your thoughts.

① Why might parents correct their children's mistakes?

② How could correcting children's mistakes upset them?

③ How can children benefit from making mistakes?

④ What harm could making mistakes do to children?

B Now, write an outline of your response based on the answers that you gave to the questions above.

Topic _____

Advantages _____

_____

Disadvantages _____

_____

Topic	Let Children Make Mistakes
Advantages	- try something and get it wrong - parents expect me to learn over time - if practice, can get better
Disadvantages	- get frustrated when make mistakes → cousin gets mad - cannot learn from mistakes → bro makes same math mistakes

C | **Using the information in the outline above, write your response here.**

_____

_____

_____

_____

_____

_____

_____

_____

_____

_____

▶ **Sample Response 1**   🎧 Q1_09_1

Let Children Make Mistakes

One advantage of letting children make mistakes is that practice makes perfect. The first time I try something, I usually do it wrong. But my parents let me make mistakes. They expect me to learn from them. Over time, by practicing, I can get better. There are also disadvantages. Some people get frustrated when they make mistakes. If my cousin does something wrong, he gets really mad. Other people simply cannot learn from their mistakes. My brother makes the same math mistakes again and again. My parents have to correct them at once. If they don't, he'll never learn.

D | **Now, say your response out loud to your partner. Don't look at your writing while you speak.**

🎧 Q1_09_3

Answer one of the following questions.

1   Some students prefer to complete their daily homework assignments at school while others prefer to finish them at their homes. Talk about the advantages and disadvantages of completing homework assignments at school. Use details and examples to explain your answer.

2   Some students prefer to complete their daily homework assignments at school while others prefer to finish them at their homes. Talk about the advantages and disadvantages of doing homework assignments at home. Use details and examples to explain your answer.

PREPARATION TIME
00:00:15

RESPONSE TIME
00:00:45

Question You are going to see a movie with some friends. Which of the following will you do to determine which movie to see?

• Read some reviews of the latest movies

• Go to the theater and make your choice there

• Let one of your friends make the decision

Use details and examples to explain your answer.

A | **Think about the following questions. Use your answers to them to help you organize your thoughts.**

Read Some Reviews	Make Your Choice at the Theater	Let a Friend Make the Decision
❶ What do movie reviews do?	❶ What can you learn about movies at a theater?	❶ Why do some people like to let others make choices for them?
❷ How much information do movie reviews give about movies?	❷ How do you feel about making choices all of a sudden?	❷ How much do you trust the opinions of your friends?

B | **Now, write an outline of your response based on the answers that you gave to the questions above.**

Your Choice _____

First Reason _____

Details _____

_____

Second Reason _____

Details _____

_____

Your Choice	Read Some Reviews
First Reason	can learn about movies
Details	- find out plots, main characters, and genres - reviewers recommend seeing or not seeing → choose good film + avoid bad ones
Second Reason	theater = expensive
Details	- don't want to waste $ on film I dislike - need to be informed about movies - spent $30 at theater once but hated movie

C | **Using the information in the outline above, write your response here.**

_____

_____

_____

_____

_____

_____

_____

_____

▶ Sample Response 1   🎧 Q1_10_1

Read Some Reviews

I will read reviews so that I can learn about movies. I can find out their plots, the main characters, and the movie genres. Reviewers also recommend seeing or not seeing films. That can help me choose a good film and avoid bad or boring ones. Secondly, going to the theater is expensive. I don't want to waste money watching a film I dislike. So it's best to be informed about the movies I can see. Once, I spent thirty dollars on tickets, popcorn, and coke. But I hated the movie. I never want to repeat that experience.

D | **Now, say your response out loud to your partner. Don't look at your writing while you speak.**

🎧 Q1_10_3

You are going to write a long paper for a school assignment. Which of the following will you do to conduct your research?

- Visit a local library and find books on the topic
- Use the Internet to do all of your research
- Contact an expert on the topic and ask that person for information

Use details and examples to explain your answer.

PREPARATION TIME
00:00:15

RESPONSE TIME
00:00:45

Part B

Integrated Speaking Tasks
Reading, Listening, and Speaking

Questions 2 & 3

◪ About the Tasks

The second and third questions require test takers to integrate different language skills. Test takers are first presented with a short reading passage. The time given for reading is 45-50 seconds. After that, test takers will listen to a conversation or a lecture which is related to information presented in the reading passage. They need to organize their response by using information from both the reading passage and the conversation or lecture. For these questions, test takers are given 30 seconds to prepare their response and 60 seconds to speak.

Question 2 concerns a topic of campus-related interest, but it does not require prior firsthand experience of college or university life in North America to understand the topic. The reading passage is usually between 75 and 100 words long. It may be an announcement, letter, or article regarding a policy, rule, or future plan of a college or university. It can also be related to campus facilities or the quality of life on campus. After reading the passage, test takers will listen to two speakers discuss the topic presented in the reading passage. Typically, one of the two speakers shows a strong opinion about the topic. Test takers need to summarize the speaker's opinion and the reasons for holding it.

In **Question 3**, test takers will read a short passage about an academic subject and then listen to a professor lecture about that subject. The question requires test takers to relate the reading passage and the lecture. Topics for this question can be drawn from a variety of fields, including life science, social science, physical science, and the humanities. However, the question does not require prior knowledge of any particular field.

When you answer the questions, be sure to use only the information that is presented in the reading passage and conversation or lecture. Even if you possess outside knowledge of the topic, you should not use it. In addition, when listening to the speakers, focus specifically on the one who is expressing a strong opinion about the topic. Ignore whatever the other person says. As for the professor, pay close attention to the examples he or she gives and then use them to show how the lecture is related to the reading passage.

VOLUME   HELP   NEXT

READING TIME 00:00:45

🎧 Q2_00_1

Library's Hours to Change

Randolph Library, the main library on campus, will be reducing its hours during the spring semester. Instead of closing at 11:00 PM on weeknights, the library will now close at 9:30 PM. On Saturday and Sunday, the library will close at 9:00 PM. The hours are being changed due to funding issues.

The man expresses his opinion about the notice by the school library. Explain his opinion and the reasons he gives for holding that opinion.

PREPARATION TIME
00:00:30

RESPONSE TIME
00:00:60

Now listen to two students discussing the notice.

M Student: How awful! Did you see this notice from the library?

W Student: No. What's going on?

M: The library's going to reduce its hours for the spring semester. It's going to be closing much earlier than normal.

W: You study there every day, don't you?

M: That's right. My roommate is pretty noisy, so I always study at the library until it closes. Now, I'm going to lose several hours of study time each week.

W: I'm so sorry to hear that, Scott.

M: You can say that again. Plus, I often meet other students there when I have group projects. I'm always busy in the afternoons and evenings, so we normally meet late at night. We'll have to find another place to meet from now on.

Sample Response 🎧 Q2_00_2

The man talks about a notice by the school library. He tells the woman that the school library's hours will be reduced. Because of a lack of money, the library will close earlier than normal on weekdays and weekends. The man is unhappy about the notice. For one thing, he mentions that he has a noisy roommate. Since he can't study in his room, he goes to the library until it closes. Now, he will study several hours fewer each week. For another thing, he often meets his group partners late at night in the library. Because of the change, he needs to find a different place to meet.

🎧 Q3_00_1

Glaciers

In some frigid places, the snow and ice do not melt. They frequently accumulate over time and then form glaciers. Glaciers are extremely heavy because they are thick and contain so much compressed snow and ice. When glaciers move forward or backward, their weight can change the landscape beneath them. Glaciers are capable of destroying mountains and can carve holes in the ground.

The professor talks about glaciated valleys and arêtes. Explain how they are related to glaciers.

PREPARATION TIME
00:00:30

RESPONSE TIME
00:00:60

Now listen to a lecture on this topic in an environmental science class.

M Professor: Thousands of years ago, this area was covered by enormous glaciers. Some were several kilometers thick. When glaciers advanced or retreated, nothing got in their way, so they dramatically changed the land's appearance.

Look at this . . . It's a picture of Yosemite National Park in California. See how the cliff is almost vertical? This picture shows a glaciated valley. Basically, uh, it formed when a glacier retreated. The glacier was so strong that it broke away large parts of the mountain, created a cliff going straight up, and formed a valley.

Now, uh, here's another landform called an arête. An arête is a narrow area of rock separating two valleys. How did it form? Well, there were glaciers on opposite sides of a mountain. While retreating, they ripped away large parts of the mountain on both sides. This created valleys on each side of the mountain. And it created the narrow strip at the top of the mountain called an arête.

Sample Response 🎧 Q3_00_2

The professor lectures on glaciated valleys and arêtes. He mentions that glaciated valleys formed when glaciers moved backward. Because the glaciers were strong, they broke off large parts of mountains. They created vertical cliffs and valleys during their retreats. The next landform the professor comments on is arêtes. They were formed when glaciers on both sides of a mountain moved backward and tore off big parts of the mountain. They created two valleys and left a narrow piece of rock at the top. Both landforms are created by glaciers. These are huge, heavy masses of snow and ice. They are able to move and can change how the land underneath them looks.

A Read the following announcement by the school gymnasium. Try to understand what the announcement is about. After reading the announcement, complete the notes below.

Gym to Close during Break

Sullivan Gymnasium will be undergoing renovations during spring break. The basketball court, locker rooms, weight room, and swimming pool will have work done on them. The entire gym will therefore be closed from March 16 to 24. Outdoor facilities such as the tennis courts will still be available for students, faculty, and staff to use.

Vocabulary
undergo ⓥ to happen; to take place
renovations ⓝ repairs, often on a building

What Will Happen _____

Details _____

_____

B Listen to a conversation about the same topic. Be sure to take notes while you listen.
🎧 Q2_01_1

Woman's Opinion _____

First Reason _____

Details _____

_____

Second Reason _____

Details _____

_____

C | Read the question and write your response by using the information in your notes.

Question The woman expresses her opinion about the announcement by the school gymnasium. Explain her opinion and the reasons she gives for holding that opinion.

_____

_____

_____

_____

_____

_____

_____

_____

_____

_____

_____

_____

D | Now, say your response out loud to your partner. Don't look at your writing while you speak.

🎧 Q2_01_3

Online Market for Students!

The student activities office is opening an online market for students. Students will be able to sell and trade various items, including books, furniture, and clothes, with one another. Only Central University students will have access to this online market. The address is www.centraluniversity.edu/onlinemarket. The market will be open for business this Saturday, September 5.

The man expresses his opinion about the announcement by the student activities office. Explain his opinion and the reasons he gives for holding that opinion.

PREPARATION TIME
00:00:30

RESPONSE TIME
00:00:60

A Read the following announcement by the Music Department. Try to understand what the announcement is about. After reading the announcement, complete the notes below.

Jazz Choir Canceled

On account of low interest, the jazz choir has been canceled. The performance scheduled for April 27 will also not be held. Those individuals who were in the jazz choir can contact the Music Department at 549-3837 to arrange to join another school choir. If there is more interest next semester, the department will consider reestablishing the jazz choir.

Vocabulary
arrange Ⓥ to make plans for; to schedule
reestablish Ⓥ to start a group or organization again

What Happened _____

Details _____

_____

_____

B Listen to a conversation about the same topic. Be sure to take notes while you listen.
🎧 Q2_02_1

Woman's Opinion _____

First Reason _____

Details _____

_____

Second Reason _____

Details _____

C | **Read the question and write your response by using the information in your notes.**

> Question The woman expresses her opinion about the announcement by the Music Department. Explain her opinion and the reasons she gives for holding that opinion.

_____

_____

_____

_____

_____

_____

_____

_____

_____

_____

_____

_____

_____

D | **Now, say your response out loud to your partner. Don't look at your writing while you speak.**

🎧 Q2_02_3

Laptop-Lending Program to End

The school's laptop-lending program, which has been in place since 2002, has been terminated. In recent years, the program has declined in popularity. The laptops used for the program will be sold. Students who do not have their own computers are encouraged to use those at the school's three computer laboratories. Visit www.easternuniversity.edu/computerlabs for more information.

The man expresses his opinion about the notice by the student services office. Explain his opinion and the reasons he gives for holding that opinion.

PREPARATION TIME
00:00:30

RESPONSE TIME
00:00:60

A Read the following letter to the editor in the school newspaper. Try to understand what the letter is about. After reading the letter, complete the notes below.

Mural Should Be Removed

The mural located on the wall at the entrance to Carpenter Gymnasium should be removed. The mural is too old and has to be constantly maintained, which is expensive. In addition, it is out of style and does not match the rest of the interior of the gym. It should be replaced by something more modern.

Sincerely,

Donald Howe

Sophomore

Vocabulary
mural *n* a painting on a wall
maintain *v* to keep in good condition

Student's Opinion _____

Details _____

B Listen to a conversation about the same topic. Be sure to take notes while you listen.
🎧 Q2_03_1

Woman's Opinion _____

First Reason _____

Details _____

Second Reason _____

Details _____

C | Read the question and write your response by using the information in your notes.

> Question The woman expresses her opinion about the letter to the editor in the school newspaper. Explain her opinion and the reasons she gives for holding that opinion.

_____

_____

_____

_____

_____

_____

_____

_____

_____

_____

_____

_____

D | Now, say your response out loud to your partner. Don't look at your writing while you speak.

VOLUME HELP NEXT

READING TIME 00:00:45

🎧 Q2_03_3

New Program for Freshmen

Freshmen will soon be able to take free buses to the downtown area on weekends. The purpose is to introduce the area to first-year students. There are numerous museums, galleries, and theaters there. Upperclassmen who guide freshmen on tours will be permitted to take the buses as well. The service will begin on January 20.

The man expresses his opinion about the notice by the student activities office. Explain his opinion and the reasons he gives for holding that opinion.

PREPARATION TIME
00:00:30

RESPONSE TIME
00:00:60

A | Read the following announcement by the Art Department. Try to understand what the announcement is about. After reading the announcement, complete the notes below.

New Program for Art Students

The stairwells in Robinson Hall, Lane Hall, and Caraway Hall are scheduled to be decorated this summer. All of the decorating will be done by students in the Art Department. Interested individuals should submit samples of their work for consideration. The art will be created in the summer and will stay up until the school year ends.

Vocabulary
stairwell *n* an area in a building that contains stairs
submit *v* to turn in; to hand in

What Will Happen _____

Details _____

B | Listen to a conversation about the same topic. Be sure to take notes while you listen.
🎧 Q2_04_1

Woman's Opinion _____

First Reason _____

Details _____

_____

Second Reason _____

Details _____

_____

C | **Read the question and write your response by using the information in your notes.**

Question The woman expresses her opinion about the announcement by the Art Department. Explain her opinion and the reasons she gives for holding that opinion.

_____

_____

_____

_____

_____

_____

_____

_____

_____

_____

_____

_____

D | **Now, say your response out loud to your partner. Don't look at your writing while you speak.**

🎧 Q2_04_3

Course Catalog to Be Upgraded

This year's course catalog will be upgraded to provide more information. The printed catalog will still only contain descriptions of the courses. But the online catalog will now include the titles of the books used in the class as well as the expected class assignments. Information about classes will be posted two months before the start of each semester.

The woman expresses her opinion about the notice by the Registrar's office. Explain her opinion and the reasons she gives for holding that opinion.

PREPARATION TIME
00:00:30

RESPONSE TIME
00:00:60

A Read the following announcement by the student services office. Try to understand what the announcement is about. After reading the announcement, complete the notes below.

Job Fair in October

There will be a job fair on Saturday, October 10. It will last from 9:00 AM to 6:00 PM and will take place in the Julian Arts Center. More than 200 domestic and international firms will be in attendance. Entry is free for all students. Please dress formally and bring multiple copies of your résumés and transcripts.

Vocabulary
domestic *adj* relating to one's own country
résumé *n* a document with information about a person such as education and work experience

What Will Happen _____

Details _____

_____

B Listen to a conversation about the same topic. Be sure to take notes while you listen.

🎧 Q2_05_1

Man's Opinion _____

First Reason _____

Details _____

_____

Second Reason _____

Details _____

_____

C | **Read the question and write your response by using the information in your notes.**

Question The man expresses his opinion about the announcement by the student services office. Explain his opinion and the reasons he gives for holding that opinion.

_____

_____

_____

_____

_____

_____

_____

_____

_____

_____

_____

_____

D | **Now, say your response out loud to your partner. Don't look at your writing while you speak.**

🎧 Q2_05_3

Hire More Economics Professors

The Economics Department is too small. Several new professors should be hired, and more classes should be offered in it. Economics is one of the most popular majors in the country. But our school only offers a few economics classes. This needs to change immediately. The students at our school ought to be able to learn more economics.

Sincerely,

Elisha Kendrick
Junior

The woman expresses her opinion about the letter to the editor in the school newspaper. Explain her opinion and the reasons she gives for holding that opinion.

PREPARATION TIME
00:00:30

RESPONSE TIME
00:00:60

A Read the following announcement by the university dining service. Try to understand what the announcement is about. After reading the announcement, complete the notes below.

Dining Hall Hours to Be Extended

All four of the university's dining halls will extend their hours of operation at night starting on November 19. Instead of closing at 7:30 PM, each dining hall will remain open until 10:00 PM. This change in hours will last until December 21. That is the last day of final exams. Please call 939-2675 if you have any questions.

Vocabulary
dining hall *n* a cafeteria; a place at a school where many students eat
hours of operation *n* the times when a store, business, building, etc. is open

What Will Happen _____

Details _____

_____

B Listen to a conversation about the same topic. Be sure to take notes while you listen.

🎧 Q2_06_1

Woman's Opinion _____

First Reason _____

Details _____

_____

Second Reason _____

Details _____

_____

C | Read the question and write your response by using the information in your notes.

> **Question** The woman expresses her opinion about the announcement by the university dining service. Explain her opinion and the reasons she gives for holding that opinion.

_____

_____

_____

_____

_____

_____

_____

_____

_____

_____

_____

D | Now, say your response out loud to your partner. Don't look at your writing while you speak.

🎧 Q2_06_3

School to Hold New Year's Festival

Once again, Coastal University will be holding a new year's festival. The festival will last from December 29 to January 2. Come to the campus to celebrate the new year. There will be plenty of entertaining games, international food, fun activities, and music shows. This year, parents are invited to attend. Admission is free. Call 685-0982 for more details.

The man expresses his opinion about the announcement by the student activities office. Explain his opinion and the reasons he gives for holding that opinion.

PREPARATION TIME
00:00:30

RESPONSE TIME
00:00:60

A   **Read the following announcement by the Registrar's office. Try to understand what the announcement is about. After reading the announcement, complete the notes below.**

New Policy on Student Transcript

Starting immediately, all students may receive two academic transcripts for free. Students may request transcripts at any time during their studies at the university. After receiving the first two transcripts at no cost, students must pay for all additional ones. The price will be $10 per transcript. Payments can be made in cash or by credit card.

Vocabulary
academic _adj_ relating to school
transcript _n_ a record of one's grades at a school

What Will Happen _____

Details _____

_____

B   **Listen to a conversation about the same topic. Be sure to take notes while you listen.**
🎧 Q2_07_1

Woman's Opinion _____

First Reason _____

Details _____

_____

Second Reason _____

Details _____

_____

C | **Read the question and write your response by using the information in your notes.**

> Question The woman expresses her opinion about the announcement by the Registrar's office. Explain her opinion and the reasons she gives for holding that opinion.

D | **Now, say your response out loud to your partner. Don't look at your writing while you speak.**

Q2_07_3

Free Fitness Class to Open

A free fitness class open to all students will start on September 4. It will take place on the grass outside the student activities center from Monday to Friday from 7:00 to 8:00 AM. In case of inclement weather, it will be held on the third floor of the building. No registration is required. Come dressed for a workout.

The woman expresses her opinion about the announcement by the student activities office. Explain her opinion and the reasons she gives for holding that opinion.

PREPARATION TIME
00:00:30

RESPONSE TIME
00:00:60

A | Read the following announcement by the dean of student's office. Try to understand what the announcement is about. After reading the announcement, complete the notes below.

New Restrictions on Student Employees

Starting in the spring semester, students will be restricted to working ten hours a week on campus. This applies to all campus jobs. If a student has two on-campus jobs, the total number of hours at both jobs may not exceed ten per week. Students should focus on their studies, not on working.

Vocabulary
restrict Ⓥ to limit something
exceed Ⓥ to go past or beyond

What Will Happen _____

Details _____

_____

_____

B | Listen to a conversation about the same topic. Be sure to take notes while you listen.
🎧 Q2_08_1

Man's Opinion _____

First Reason _____

Details _____

_____

Second Reason _____

Details _____

_____

C | Read the question and write your response by using the information in your notes.

Question The man expresses his opinion about the announcement by the dean of student's office. Explain his opinion and the reasons he gives for holding that opinion.

D | Now, say your response out loud to your partner. Don't look at your writing while you speak.

🎧 Q2_08_3

Performing Arts Exhibition Postponed

The date of the Wildwoods Performing Arts Exhibition has been changed. It will no longer be held from November 10 to 14. Instead, it will take place from December 2 to 6. The exhibition is being moved due to a scheduling conflict involving Davidson Hall, the location of the event. Interested individuals should call 777-9238 for more information.

The woman expresses her opinion about the announcement by the Drama Department. Explain her opinion and the reasons she gives for holding that opinion.

PREPARATION TIME
00:00:30

RESPONSE TIME
00:00:60

A Read the following advertisement by the Music Department. Try to understand what the advertisement is about. After reading the advertisement, complete the notes below.

Come and Enjoy Some Classical Music

From October 1 to December 10, enjoy classical music on the weekend. The school orchestra will perform every Saturday evening starting at 7:00 PM. Be sure to visit the theater in Carter Hall. Admission is free to students, faculty, and staff members. Come by to support the school orchestra and to hear some masterpieces of classical music.

Vocabulary
admission ⓝ right or permission to enter a place
masterpiece ⓝ a great work

What Will Happen _____

Details _____

_____

B Listen to a conversation about the same topic. Be sure to take notes while you listen.
🎧 Q2_09_1

Man's Opinion _____

First Reason _____

Details _____

_____

Second Reason _____

Details _____

_____

C | Read the question and write your response by using the information in your notes.

> **Question** The man expresses his opinion about the advertisement by the Music Department. Explain his opinion and the reasons he gives for holding that opinion.

_____

_____

_____

_____

_____

_____

_____

_____

_____

_____

_____

D | Now, say your response out loud to your partner. Don't look at your writing while you speak.

🎧 Q2_09_3

No More Tours at University Art Museum

No more tours of the Fuller Art Museum will take place this semester. Tours are given by professors in the Art History Department. However, due to their increased workloads, the professors no longer have any free time. Guests are still welcome to visit the museum during its hours of operation. The museum is open daily from 1:00 to 6:00 PM.

The man expresses his opinion about the announcement by the Art History Department. Explain his opinion and the reasons he gives for holding that opinion.

PREPARATION TIME
00:00:30

RESPONSE TIME
00:00:60

A Read the following announcement by the Registrar's office. Try to understand what the announcement is about. After reading the announcement, complete the notes below.

New Date for Dropping Classes

The date for dropping classes has been changed. Students must now drop classes no later than September 15. All drop forms must be submitted to the Registrar's office by 6:00 PM on that day. A completed drop form should have the class professor's and student advisor's signatures. Drop forms may be downloaded from the university website.

Vocabulary
drop Ⓥ to stop taking a class
advisor Ⓝ a person who gives advice or help to another

What Will Happen _____

Details _____

_____

B Listen to a conversation about the same topic. Be sure to take notes while you listen.
🎧 Q2_10_1

Woman's Opinion _____

First Reason _____

Details _____

_____

Second Reason _____

Details _____

_____

C | **Read the question and write your response by using the information in your notes.**

> Question The woman expresses her opinion about the announcement by the Registrar's office. Explain her opinion and the reasons she gives for holding that opinion.

_____

_____

_____

_____

_____

_____

_____

_____

_____

_____

_____

_____

D | **Now, say your response out loud to your partner. Don't look at your writing while you speak.**

🎧 Q2_10_3

Pay Student Volunteers

I'm pleased the school has opened a botanical garden full of numerous species of plants. Many students in the Biology Department worked hard to make it a beautiful garden. No students have been paid though. I encourage the school to pay these students. The school can use donations to the university to pay student volunteers an hourly wage.

Christina Ripple
Senior

The man expresses his opinion about the letter to the editor in the school newspaper. Explain his opinion and the reasons he gives for holding that opinion.

PREPARATION TIME
00:00:30

RESPONSE TIME
00:00:60

A | Read the following passage. Try to understand what the passage is about. After reading the passage, complete the notes below.

Animal Communication

Animals are capable of communicating both verbally and nonverbally. Verbal communication involves making sounds. For example, dogs bark whereas cats meow. Animals may also grunt, hiss, and make many other types of noises to express themselves. Nonverbal communication involves using body language. For instance, animals may show their teeth to express anger. They may wag their tails to show happiness as well.

Vocabulary
grunt 🔽 to make a deep sound like a pig
wag 🔽 to move back and forth, often quickly

Main Idea of the Passage _____

Details _____

_____

B | Listen to part of a lecture about the same topic. Be sure to take notes while you listen.
🎧 Q3_01_1

Thesis Statement _____

First Example _____

Details _____

_____

Second Example _____

Details _____

_____

C | Read the question and write your response by using the information in your notes.

> **Question** The professor talks about her cat. Explain how her cat's actions are related to animal communication.

_____

_____

_____

_____

_____

_____

_____

_____

_____

_____

_____

D | Now, say your response out loud to your partner. Don't look at your writing while you speak.

Q3_01_3

Specialization

Humans are able to perform a wide variety of tasks. However, countless animals practice specialization. As a result, they can only do a limited number of tasks. Specialization is common for insects. Each insect has a specific role in its colony. This allows all of them to work in the most efficient manner. This helps the insect colony be as successful as possible.

The professor talks about ants. Explain how their actions are related to specialization.

PREPARATION TIME
00:00:30

RESPONSE TIME
00:00:60

A | Read the following passage. Try to understand what the passage is about. After reading the passage, complete the notes below.

Discipline

Discipline is utilized to regulate behavior. When a person breaks a rule or acts improperly, that individual must be disciplined. This can be accomplished in various ways. It may involve verbal or physical punishment or restrict a person's rights. It can result in the loss of possessions for a certain amount of time. A person may also be imprisoned and spend time in jail.

Vocabulary
regulate Ⓥ to control
imprison Ⓥ to put into jail so that a person cannot leave for a certain amount of time

Main Idea of the Passage _____

Details _____

_____

_____

_____

B | Listen to part of a lecture about the same topic. Be sure to take notes while you listen.
🎧 Q3_02_1

Thesis Statement _____

Example _____

Details _____

_____

_____

_____

_____

C | **Read the question and write your response by using the information in your notes.**

Question The professor talks about her daughter. Explain how the professor's and her daughter's actions are related to discipline.

_____

_____

_____

_____

_____

_____

_____

_____

_____

_____

_____

_____

D | **Now, say your response out loud to your partner. Don't look at your writing while you speak.**

iBT Practice Test

VOLUME

HELP

NEXT

Question 3 of 4

READING TIME 00:00:45

🎧 Q3_02_3

Generalizations

People often make broad statements about groups of people or things. These statements usually have some truth to them. However, they are not always true or accurate for specific people or things. These generalizations may be statements like "All dogs hate cats" or "It always snows in winter." Most of the time, people generalize without considering the possible exceptions to their statements.

The professor talks about visiting his brother. Explain how his experiences during his visit are related to generalizations.

PREPARATION TIME
00:00:30

RESPONSE TIME
00:00:60

A | **Read the following passage. Try to understand what the passage is about. After reading the passage, complete the notes below.**

Camouflage

Some animals are difficult for others to see. They may have colors or stripes that enable them to hide in their natural environment. They may resemble objects such as rocks, leaves, tree bark, or branches, too. These are all forms of camouflage. Camouflage lets animals hide from others. Some use it to protect themselves from predators while others use it to catch prey more easily.

Vocabulary
tree bark *n* the hard, tough outer covering of a tree
prey *n* an animal that is hunted by other animals

Main Idea of the Passage _____

Details _____

_____

_____

B | **Listen to part of a lecture about the same topic. Be sure to take notes while you listen.**
 Q3_03_1

Thesis Statement _____

First Example _____

Details _____

_____

Second Example _____

Details _____

_____

C | Read the question and write your response by using the information in your notes.

> **Question** The professor talks about polar bears and snapping turtles. Explain how they are related to camouflage.

_____

_____

_____

_____

_____

_____

_____

_____

_____

_____

_____

_____

D | Now, say your response out loud to your partner. Don't look at your writing while you speak.

🎧 Q3_03_3

Animal Overpopulation

The population of an animal species sometimes increases greatly. Whenever this occurs, overpopulation happens. There are typically several results of overpopulation. The food supply decreases because more animals are eating the available food. In addition, there is not enough space for all of the animals to live. In many instances, large numbers of them die because their numbers are too great.

The professor talks about the rabbits in the forest. Explain how they are related to animal overpopulation.

PREPARATION TIME
00:00:30

RESPONSE TIME
00:00:60

A Read the following passage. Try to understand what the passage is about. After reading the passage, complete the notes below.

Opportunity Cost

Sometimes a person may have to make a choice between doing one of two different things. For instance, perhaps an individual has $1,000. The person can either go on a trip abroad or purchase a new computer. The opportunity cost is the value of the purchase the person does not make. If the person takes the trip, the opportunity cost is the computer.

Vocabulary
abroad *adv* to or in another country
value *n* a price; the worth of something

Main Idea of the Passage _____

Details _____

_____

B Listen to part of a lecture about the same topic. Be sure to take notes while you listen.

🎧 Q3_04_1

Thesis Statement _____

Example _____

Details _____

_____

_____

_____

_____

C | **Read the question and write your response by using the information in your notes.**

Question The professor talks about a donation to the city. Explain how it is related to opportunity cost.

_____

_____

_____

_____

_____

_____

_____

_____

_____

_____

_____

_____

_____

D | **Now, say your response out loud to your partner. Don't look at your writing while you speak.**

🎧 Q3_04_3

The Trickle-Down Effect

In most societies, fashion leaders belong to the upper class. These people determine what is popular. Over time, the members of the lower classes develop the same tastes as the members of the upper classes. The tastes of the upper class basically trickle down to the lower classes. Then, the upper class changes the styles it prefers to be different from the lower classes.

The professor talks about Lacoste and Burberry. Explain how they are related to the trickle-down effect.

PREPARATION TIME
00:00:30

RESPONSE TIME
00:00:60

A | Read the following passage. Try to understand what the passage is about. After reading the passage, complete the notes below.

Warning Coloration

Some animals are brightly colored or have distinct markings on parts of their bodies. The bright colors are normally red, orange, and yellow. The colors and markings make the animals easy to see. They serve as warnings to predators. In most cases, animals using warning coloration are poisonous or dangerous in some manner. Predators recognize this, so they do not attack these animals.

Vocabulary
distinct *adj* obvious; easy to see
recognize *v* to notice; to see

Main Idea of the Passage _____

Details _____

_____

B | Listen to part of a lecture about the same topic. Be sure to take notes while you listen.
🎧 Q3_05_1

Thesis Statement _____

First Example _____

Details _____

_____

_____

Second Example _____

Details _____

_____

_____

C | **Read the question and write your response by using the information in your notes.**

> Question The professor talks about the tiger moth and the coral snake. Explain how their actions are related to warning coloration.

_____

_____

_____

_____

_____

_____

_____

_____

_____

_____

_____

_____

D | **Now, say your response out loud to your partner. Don't look at your writing while you speak.**

🎧 Q3_05_3

Harmony

Some animals live in large groups with family members or unrelated animals. It is necessary for these animals to have peaceful relations with one another. When they maintain harmony, the entire group can prosper. To have harmonious relationships, the animals may do activities that cause them to rely on one another to prosper. Others may engage in activities that are distracting at times.

The professor talks about monkeys. Explain how their actions are related to harmony.

PREPARATION TIME
00:00:30

RESPONSE TIME
00:00:60

A | **Read the following passage. Try to understand what the passage is about. After reading the passage, complete the notes below.**

Metamorphosis

Some animals undergo rapid changes in their bodies after they are born or hatched. These changes may involve how many arms or legs they have, how they look, and how they are able to breathe. As a result, these animals typically look much different after metamorphosis than they did before undergoing the process. Fish, insects, amphibians, and mollusks sometimes undergo metamorphosis.

Vocabulary
amphibian *n* a class of animals that can live both in the water and on land
mollusk *n* a group of animals with shells that includes squid, snails, and octopuses

Main Idea of the Passage _____

Details _____

_____

B | **Listen to part of a lecture about the same topic. Be sure to take notes while you listen.**
🎧 Q3_06_1

Example _____

Details _____

_____

_____

_____

_____

C | **Read the question and write your response by using the information in your notes.**

> Question The professor talks about tadpoles. Explain how they are related to metamorphosis.

_____

_____

_____

_____

_____

_____

_____

_____

_____

_____

_____

D | **Now, say your response out loud to your partner. Don't look at your writing while you speak.**

🎧 Q3_06_3

Empty Nest Syndrome

When children move away from home, their parents sometimes experience feelings of sadness and loneliness. They may even become highly depressed and feel a strong sense of grief. This happens because their children are no longer living at home. Many parents encourage their children to become independent. Nevertheless, the shock of their children suddenly being gone creates strong negative emotions in parents.

The professor talks about her friend's experience with her son. Explain how it is related to empty nest syndrome.

PREPARATION TIME
00:00:30

RESPONSE TIME
00:00:60

A | Read the following passage. Try to understand what the passage is about. After reading the passage, complete the notes below.

Crop Rotation

Some farmers plant different crops on the same land in subsequent years. Sometimes they plant no crops at all in their fields. They do this to improve the condition of the soil. Certain plants remove nutrients from the soil while others restore nutrients. By practicing crop rotation, farmers can avoid removing essential nutrients from the soil and making it worthless.

Vocabulary
subsequent *adj* happening later or after something
essential *adj* very important

Main Idea of the Passage _____

Details _____

_____

B | Listen to part of a lecture about the same topic. Be sure to take notes while you listen.
🎧 Q3_07_1

Thesis Statement _____

Example _____

Details _____

_____

_____

_____

_____

C | Read the question and write your response by using the information in your notes.

> Question The professor talks about the three-field system. Explain how it is related to crop rotation.

D | Now, say your response out loud to your partner. Don't look at your writing while you speak.

🎧 Q3_07_3

Handedness

Most people have a dominant hand. This is the hand which they prefer to use for a variety of activities. Among them are writing, eating, and throwing things. People are typically more precise and do activities faster with their dominant hand. Around ninety percent of humans are righthanded. A much smaller number of people are lefthanded.

The professor talks about the red kangaroo. Explain how it is related to handedness.

PREPARATION TIME
00:00:30

RESPONSE TIME
00:00:60

A | Read the following passage. Try to understand what the passage is about. After reading the passage, complete the notes below.

Automation

Automation refers to the act of using machines to do work in place of humans. These machines are electronic or mechanical devices. They require a low level—or no level—of human involvement. Instead, they can work automatically without being observed or operated by humans. Automation is becoming common in places around the world.

Vocabulary
device *n* something made for a certain purpose
involvement *n* the act of being included in an activity, group, etc.

Main Idea of the Passage _____

Details _____

_____

B | Listen to part of a lecture about the same topic. Be sure to take notes while you listen.
🎧 Q3_08_1

Example _____

Details _____

_____

_____

_____

_____

_____

C | **Read the question and write your response by using the information in your notes.**

> Question The professor talks about a new factory being built. Explain how it is related to automation.

D | **Now, say your response out loud to your partner. Don't look at your writing while you speak.**

Q3_08_3

Duper's Delight

Some people enjoy duping, or tricking, others. They may gain feelings of power over others when they fool people. However, many dupers cannot hide their feelings. Their bodies frequently give off signals that they are being dishonest. For instance, dupers may show their delight by smiling. Their eyes may squint, they may bite their lips, and they may throw their heads back as well.

The professor talks about her experiences with a used car salesman and a student. Explain how they are related to duper's delight.

PREPARATION TIME
00:00:30

RESPONSE TIME
00:00:60

A Read the following passage. Try to understand what the passage is about. After reading the passage, complete the notes below.

Parasitism

Sometimes two species have a long-term relationship. Because of it, one species benefits from the other. However, the other species is harmed in the process. In some cases, the harmed species suffers mild pain. In other cases, that species is greatly injured or even killed. The parasite—the species doing the harming—is sometimes unable to survive without a host.

Vocabulary
harm *v* to hurt or damage something
mild *adj* not strong or serious

Main Idea of the Passage _____

Details _____

_____

B Listen to part of a lecture about the same topic. Be sure to take notes while you listen.
Q3_09_1

Example _____

Details _____

_____

_____

_____

_____

_____

C | Read the question and write your response by using the information in your notes.

> **Question** The professor talks about fleas. Explain how they are related to parasitism.

D | Now, say your response out loud to your partner. Don't look at your writing while you speak.

iBT Practice Test

Question 3 of 4

VOLUME

HELP

NEXT

READING TIME 00:00:45

🎧 Q3_09_3

Recall Bias

When people self-report about events in their past, they sometimes suffer from recall bias. This happens for two primary reasons. The people may fail to remember an event or activity in their past accurately. Therefore, they report false information by accident. In other cases, people knowingly omit information or even lie about their past activities. They are usually too embarrassed to tell the truth.

The professor talks about her brother and sister. Explain how they are related to recall bias.

PREPARATION TIME
00:00:30

RESPONSE TIME
00:00:60

A | **Read the following passage. Try to understand what the passage is about. After reading the passage, complete the notes below.**

Fermentation

This is a process in which food is altered from its original state. Microorganisms such as yeast and bacteria are necessary for this process to work. They take carbohydrates such as starch and sugar in foods and change them into either alcohol or acids. The alcohol and the acids both help preserve the foods and give them a tart taste.

Vocabulary
yeast *n* a type of fungus used to help bread rise and to make alcohol
microorganism *n* any living creature too small to be seen without a microscope

Main Idea of the Passage _____

Details _____

_____

B | **Listen to part of a lecture about the same topic. Be sure to take notes while you listen.**
🎧 Q3_10_1

Example _____

Details _____

_____

_____

_____

_____

_____

C | **Read the question and write your response by using the information in your notes.**

> Question The professor talks about yogurt. Explain how it is related to fermentation.

_____

_____

_____

_____

_____

_____

_____

_____

_____

_____

_____

_____

D | **Now, say your response out loud to your partner. Don't look at your writing while you speak.**

🎧 Q3_10_3

Poisoning the Well Fallacy

When two people engage in a debate, they may resort to using logical fallacies. One such fallacy is called poisoning the well. The person using it attacks the other individual with irrelevant information. The person presents negative information about the other in an attempt to discredit that individual. People who use this fallacy properly make it difficult for a person to respond to their attacks.

The professor talks about a recent political debate. Explain how it is related to the poisoning the well fallacy.

PREPARATION TIME
00:00:30

RESPONSE TIME
00:00:60

◢ About the Task

The last question presents only a listening passage—a lecture—and not a reading passage. Test takers need to respond based on what they heard. They are given 20 seconds to prepare their response and 60 seconds to speak.

For **Question 4**, test takers will listen to a lecture about an academic topic. As in Question 3, topics for this question can be drawn from a variety of fields, including life science, social science, physical science, and the humanities. Again, no prior knowledge is necessary to understand the lecture. After hearing the lecture, test takers are asked to summarize the lecture and to explain how the examples are connected with the overall topic.

When you answer this question, be sure to focus on what the professor discusses. All of the information you discuss should come from the professor's talk. Even if you possess outside knowledge of the topic, you should not use it. Instead, focus solely on the information that the professor provides and then explain how it relates to the question.

VOLUME HELP NEXT

Q4_00_1

Using points and examples from the talk, explain two advantages of paperless offices.

PREPARATION TIME
00:00:20

RESPONSE TIME
00:00:60

Listen to part of a lecture in a business class.

M Professor: Thanks to computers and modern technology, countless companies are transitioning to paperless offices. Essentially, they decrease the amount of paper they use by putting their documents onto computers and into electronic form. As you know, I'm a part-time instructor here, and I happen to work in a paperless office full time. There are, um, quite a few benefits.

One is that it's simple to share documents with others. When one of my colleagues wants a report, a contract, or an application form, I simply email it. In the past, I had to use the copy machine and then physically hand the paper to my coworker. Nowadays, it takes virtually no time to transfer documents, uh, even if I'm sending them to the other side of the world.

Another advantage is that companies save money. Think about it . . . When offices put documents online, they need less paper and ink. They save money on toner and need fewer copy machines and printers, too. They can also rent less space because they don't have to store so many physical documents. My company saves more than $60,000 a year because we're almost entirely paperless.

Q4_00_2

The professor tells the students that there are many advantages to paperless offices. These are offices where most of the documents are stored on computers and in electronic form. One advantage he mentions is that it's easy to share documents. When someone needs a document, he doesn't have to copy it and give it to that person. Instead, he just emails it instantly. A second advantage he discusses is that paperless offices save money. There are reduced costs because companies save on paper, ink, toner, copy machines, and printers. The professor remarks that his company saves $60,000 a year because it is a paperless office.

A | **Listen to a lecture on zoology. Be sure to take notes while you listen.** 🎧 Q4_01_1

Main Topic _____

Main Idea _____

First Example _____

Details _____

_____

_____

_____

_____

Second Example _____

Details _____

_____

_____

_____

_____

Vocabulary

☐ **be familiar with** *phr* to know about

☐ **detect** *v* to find; to see

☐ **home in on** *phr* to track; to find the location of a place and then to go there

☐ **maximum** *adj* greatest in amount or number

☐ **mate** *v* to reproduce; to make offspring

☐ **larva** *n* an insect that has just emerged from an egg

☐ **hatch** *v* to come out from an egg

☐ **consume** *v* to eat

B Read the question and write your response by using the information in your notes.

> Question Using points and examples from the talk, explain the importance of heat to mosquitoes and charcoal beetles.

_____

_____

_____

_____

_____

_____

_____

_____

_____

_____

_____

_____

_____

C Now, say your response out loud to your partner. Don't look at your writing while you speak.

🎧 Q4_01_3

Using points and examples from the talk, explain two types of defenses against predators that caterpillars use.

PREPARATION TIME

00:00:20

RESPONSE TIME

00:00:60

A | **Listen to a lecture on anthropology. Be sure to take notes while you listen.** 🎧 Q4_02_1

Main Topic _____

Main Idea _____

First Way _____

Details _____

_____

_____

_____

_____

Second Way _____

Details _____

_____

_____

_____

_____

Vocabulary

☐ **devise** *v* to create; to think of

☐ **spoil** *v* to go bad, like food

☐ **cultivate** *v* to grow crops or other plants

☐ **vast** *adj* very large in amount or number

☐ **flow** *v* to move like air or water

☐ **chunk** *n* a large piece of something

☐ **secure** *v* to tie one thing to another to keep it from moving

☐ **edible** *adj* able to be eaten

B | **Read the question and write your response by using the information in your notes.**

> Question Using points and examples from the talk, explain two ways that people in ancient cultures preserved food.

_____

_____

_____

_____

_____

_____

_____

_____

_____

_____

_____

C | **Now, say your response out loud to your partner. Don't look at your writing while you speak.**

Q4_02_3

Using points and examples from the talk, explain two ways that ancient societies developed solidarity.

PREPARATION TIME
00:00:20

RESPONSE TIME
00:00:60

Question 4 #3

A | **Listen to a lecture on marketing. Be sure to take notes while you listen.** 🎧 Q4_03_1

Main Topic _____

Main Idea _____

What the Professor Did _____

Details _____

_____

_____

_____

How the Campaign Went _____

Details _____

_____

_____

_____

_____

Vocabulary

☐ **advertise** _v_ to promote a good or service in order to sell it

☐ **sneakers** _n_ sports shoes; tennis shoes

☐ **professional** _adj_ doing a certain job or occupation for money

☐ **athlete** _n_ a person who plays sports

☐ **enormous** _adj_ very large or great

☐ **campaign** _n_ a promotion; an event

☐ **wind up** _phr_ to have a certain result

☐ **profit** _n_ money that a person or group earns

B | **Read the question and write your response by using the information in your notes.**

Question Using points and examples from the talk, explain how the professor used viral marketing to sell a product.

_____

_____

_____

_____

_____

_____

_____

_____

_____

_____

_____

C | **Now, say your response out loud to your partner. Don't look at your writing while you speak.**

iBT Practice Test

Question 4 of 4

VOLUME

HELP

NEXT

READING TIME 00:00:45

🎧 Q4_03_3

Using points and examples from the talk, explain two ways that internal constraints hurt the company where the professor used to work.

PREPARATION TIME
00:00:20

RESPONSE TIME
00:00:60

A | **Listen to a lecture on botany. Be sure to take notes while you listen.** 🎧 Q4_04_1

Main Topic _____

Main Idea _____

First Example _____

Details _____

_____

_____

_____

Second Example _____

Details _____

_____

_____

_____

_____

Vocabulary

☐ **deal with** *phr* to handle

☐ **pesticide** *n* a type of poison that kills insects

☐ **eliminate** *v* to kill

☐ **beneficial** *adj* helpful

☐ **attract** *v* to cause something to go to another thing

☐ **devour** *v* to eat

☐ **nectar** *n* a sweet liquid that some plants produce

☐ **parasite** *n* the cover formed by the leaves of trees in a forest

B | **Read the question and write your response by using the information in your notes.**

> Question Using points and examples from the talk, explain how some plants can attract beneficial insects.

_____

_____

_____

_____

_____

_____

_____

_____

_____

_____

_____

C | **Now, say your response out loud to your partner. Don't look at your writing while you speak.**

🎧 Q4_04_3

Using points and examples from the talk, explain two ways that seeds germinate.

PREPARATION TIME
00:00:20

RESPONSE TIME
00:00:60

A | **Listen to a lecture on zoology. Be sure to take notes while you listen.** 🎧 Q4_05_1

Main Topic _____

Main Idea _____

First Example _____

Details _____

_____

_____

_____

_____

Second Example _____

Details _____

_____

_____

_____

_____

Vocabulary

☐ **numerous** *adj* great or many in amount or number

☐ **flee** *v* to run away

☐ **lock** *v* to put in a position so that something cannot move

☐ **muscles** *n* cells in the body that are responsible for movement

☐ **expend** *v* to use

☐ **burst** *n* a short period in which something is done, often quickly

☐ **alert** *adj* awake and aware

☐ **impression** *n* an appearance

B | Read the question and write your response by using the information in your notes.

> Question Using points and examples from the talk, explain how giraffes and deer avoid predators while sleeping.

_____

_____

_____

_____

_____

_____

_____

_____

_____

_____

_____

_____

C | Now, say your response out loud to your partner. Don't look at your writing while you speak.

🎧 Q4_05_3

Using points and examples from the talk, explain why foxes and eagles have excellent vision.

PREPARATION TIME

00:00:20

RESPONSE TIME

00:00:60

A | **Listen to a lecture on astronomy. Be sure to take notes while you listen.** 🎧 Q4_06_1

Main Topic _____

Main Idea _____

First Example _____

Details _____

_____

_____

_____

Second Example _____

Details _____

_____

_____

_____

_____

Vocabulary

☐ **solar system** *n* the sun and everything in space that orbits it

☐ **positive** *adj* sure

☐ **collide** *v* to run into; to hit

☐ **debris** *n* the remains of something that has been destroyed

☐ **cast** *v* to throw, often very far

☐ **spherical** *adj* shaped like a circle

☐ **asteroid** *n* a large rock that orbits the sun

☐ **gravitational force** *n* the force that causes objects to be attracted to one another

B | **Read the question and write your response by using the information in your notes.**

> Question Using points and examples from the talk, explain two ways that moons in the solar system formed.

_____

_____

_____

_____

_____

_____

_____

_____

_____

_____

_____

_____

C | **Now, say your response out loud to your partner. Don't look at your writing while you speak.**

🎧 Q4_06_3

Using points and examples from the talk, explain two reasons that mangrove trees are unique.

PREPARATION TIME
00:00:20

RESPONSE TIME
00:00:60

A | **Listen to a lecture on botany. Be sure to take notes while you listen.** 🎧 Q4_07_1

Main Idea _____

Details _____

_____

First Example _____

Details _____

_____

_____

_____

_____

Second Example _____

Details _____

_____

_____

_____

_____

Vocabulary

☐ **fertilization** *n* the act of making a plant able to reproduce

☐ **pollinate** *v* to transfer pollen from one part of a flower to another so that it can reproduce

☐ **blossom** *n* a flower on a plant

☐ **attract** *v* to cause or make something come closer to oneself

☐ **ultraviolet** *adj* relating to the colors beyond violet on the color spectrum

☐ **spectrum** *n* a band or series of colors

☐ **enormous** *adj* very large; huge

☐ **corpse** *n* a dead body

B | **Read the question and write your response by using the information in your notes.**

> Question Using points and examples from the talk, explain two ways that plants attract animal pollinators.

_____

_____

_____

_____

_____

_____

_____

_____

_____

_____

_____

_____

C | **Now, say your response out loud to your partner. Don't look at your writing while you speak.**

iBT Practice Test

Question 4 of 4

VOLUME

HELP

NEXT

READING TIME 00:00:45

🎧 Q4_07_3

Using points and examples from the talk, explain two disadvantages of process standardization.

PREPARATION TIME
00:00:20

RESPONSE TIME
00:00:60

A | **Listen to a lecture on environmental science. Be sure to take notes while you listen.**

🎧 Q4_08_1

Main Topic _____

Main Idea _____

First Way _____

Details _____

_____

_____

_____

_____

Second Way _____

Details _____

_____

_____

_____

_____

_____

Vocabulary

- ☐ **tanker** *n* a ship that transports oil
- ☐ **severely** *adv* very much; greatly
- ☐ **skimmer** *n* a device that removes matter from the top of a liquid
- ☐ **boom** *n* a floating barrier that prevents oil from spreading
- ☐ **suck up** *v* to draw in by using a vacuum
- ☐ **dispersant** *n* something that causes another thing to break up
- ☐ **spray** *v* to scatter a liquid by shooting fine particles of it
- ☐ **marine** *adj* relating to the ocean

B | Read the question and write your response by using the information in your notes.

> Question Using points and examples from the talk, explain two ways that oil spills can be removed from the ocean.

_____

_____

_____

_____

_____

_____

_____

_____

_____

_____

_____

_____

C | Now, say your response out loud to your partner. Don't look at your writing while you speak.

iBT Practice Test

VOLUME

HELP

NEXT

Question 4 of 4

READING TIME 00:00:45

🎧 Q4_08_3

Using points and examples from the talk, explain two reasons that the professor supports vertical farming.

PREPARATION TIME
00:00:20

RESPONSE TIME
00:00:60

A | **Listen to a lecture on chemistry. Be sure to take notes while you listen.** 🎧 Q4_09_1

Main Topic _____

Main Idea _____

First Method _____

Details _____

_____

_____

_____

_____

Second Method _____

Details _____

_____

_____

_____

_____

▌ Vocabulary

☐ **dating method** *n* a way to tell how old something is

☐ **trunk** *n* the thick stem of a tree

☐ **determine** *v* to figure out or learn

☐ **overlap** *v* to have in common with

☐ **accurately** *adv* correctly

☐ **lakebed** *n* the bottom of a lake

☐ **peat bog** *n* a swamp with lots of partially decayed vegetation

☐ **fossilize** *v* to replace organic matter with minerals to make something a fossil

B | **Read the question and write your response by using the information in your notes.**

Question Using points and examples from the talk, explain two dating methods that scientists use.

_____

_____

_____

_____

_____

_____

_____

_____

_____

_____

_____

_____

C | **Now, say your response out loud to your partner. Don't look at your writing while you speak.**

Using points and examples from the talk, explain two methods that companies use to reduce the number of options their customers have to choose from.

PREPARATION TIME
00:00:20

RESPONSE TIME
00:00:60

A | **Listen to a lecture on botany. Be sure to take notes while you listen.** 🎧 Q4_10_1

Main Topic _____

Main Idea _____

Details _____

First Example _____

Details _____

_____

_____

_____

_____

Second Example _____

Details _____

_____

_____

_____

_____

Vocabulary

- ☐ **invasive** *adj* posing a threat to an area by growing or reproducing quickly
- ☐ **ecosystem** *n* a group of interconnected elements and the area that they are in
- ☐ **disrupt** *v* to destroy, break apart, or cause problems
- ☐ **climate** *n* the general weather conditions in an area
- ☐ **shade** *n* darkness caused when the sun's light is blocked in a place
- ☐ **crowd out** *v* to push or shove away
- ☐ **dense** *adj* thick
- ☐ **canopy** *n* the cover formed by the leaves of trees in a forest

B | **Read the question and write your response by using the information in your notes.**

Question Using points and examples from the talk, explain how English ivy and the Norway maple tree are invasive species.

_____

_____

_____

_____

_____

_____

_____

_____

_____

_____

_____

_____

C | **Now, say your response out loud to your partner. Don't look at your writing while you speak.**

Q4_10_3

Using points and examples from the talk, explain two ways that taking breaks at work can benefit employees.

PREPARATION TIME
00 : 00 : 20

RESPONSE TIME
00 : 00 : 60

Actual Test

AT00

Speaking Section Directions

🎧 **Make sure your headset is on.**

This section measures your ability to speak about a variety of topics. You will answer four questions by speaking into the microphone. Answer as completely as possible.

In the first question, you will speak about familiar topics. Your response will be scored on your ability to speak clearly and coherently.

In the next two questions, you will first read a short reading passage. This passage will go away, and you will then listen to a talk on the same topic. You will be asked about the information you have read and heard. You will need to combine information from the reading passage and the talk to provide a complete answer. Your response will be scored on your ability to speak clearly and coherently and how accurately you convey information about what you read and heard.

In the last question, you will listen to part of a lecture. You will be asked about what you have heard. Your response will be scored on your ability to speak clearly and coherently and how accurately you convey information about what you heard.

You may take notes while you read and while you listen to the conversations and lectures. You may use your notes to help prepare your response.

Listen carefully to the directions for each question. The directions will not be written on the screen.

For each question, you will be given a short time to prepare your response (15 to 30 seconds, depending on the question). A clock will show how much preparation time is remaining. When the preparation time is up, you will be told to begin your response. A clock will show how much response time is remaining. A message will appear on the screen when the response time has ended.

🎧 AT01

Do you agree or disagree with the following statement?

Public transportation such as buses and subways should be free for everyone.

Please include specific examples and details to support your explanation.

PREPARATION TIME
00:00:15

RESPONSE TIME
00:00:45

AT02

Undergraduate Teaching Assistants Now Accepted

Undergraduates may now apply to become teaching assistants for classes. Only juniors and seniors are eligible. Applicants must have a minimum GPA of 3.30 and a GPA of 3.60 or higher in their majors. Interested students should apply directly to the professors they want to TA for. Successful individuals will be paid the same as graduate students.

The man expresses his opinion about the announcement by the dean of students. Explain his opinion and the reasons he gives for holding that opinion.

PREPARATION TIME
00:00:30

RESPONSE TIME
00:00:60

AT03

The Generation Effect

Information is often hard for people to remember. This is especially true when they merely read the information. In many cases, people quickly forget what they read. However, when people engage in active learning, their memories improve. Psychologists have noticed that when individuals generate information in their minds, they tend to remember it better. They can therefore retain the knowledge in their long-term memory.

The professor talks about an experiment a psychologist conducted. Explain how it is related to the generation effect.

PREPARATION TIME
00:00:30

RESPONSE TIME
00:00:60

🎧 AT04

Using points and examples from the talk, explain how maximizers and satisficers behave.

PREPARATION TIME
00:00:20

RESPONSE TIME
00:00:60

Authors

Michael A. Putlack
- MA in History, Tufts University, Medford, MA, USA
- Expert test developer of TOEFL, TOEIC, and TEPS
- Main author of the Darakwon *How to Master Skills for the TOEFL® iBT* series and *TOEFL® MAP* series

Stephen Poirier
- Candidate for PhD in History, University of Western Ontario, Canada
- Certificate of Professional Technical Writing, Carleton University, Canada
- Co-author of the Darakwon *How to Master Skills for the TOEFL® iBT* series and *TOEFL® MAP* series

Tony Covello
- BA in Political Science, Beloit College, Beloit, WI, USA
- MA in TEFL, International Graduate School of English, Seoul, Korea
- Term instructor at George Mason University Korea, Songdo, Incheon, Korea

Decoding the TOEFL® iBT
SPEAKING Basic NEW TOEFL® EDITION

Publisher Chung Kyudo
Editor Kim Minju
Authors Michael A. Putlack, Stephen Poirier, Tony Covello
Proofreader Michael A. Putlack
Designers Koo Soojung, Park Sunyoung

First published in May 2021
By Darakwon, Inc.
Darakwon Bldg., 211, Munbal-ro, Paju-si, Gyeonggi-do 10881
Republic of Korea
Tel: 82-2-736-2031 (Ext. 250)
Fax: 82-2-732-2037

ISBN 978-89-277-0878-0 14740
       978-89-277-0875-9 14740 (set)

www.darakwon.co.kr

Components Student Book / Answer Book
8 7 6 5 4 3 2   23 24 25 26 27